Wisconsin

BY HOLLY SAARI

The Child's World

Published by The Child's World®
1980 Lookout Drive • Mankato, MN 56003-1705
800-599-READ • www.childsworld.com

ACKNOWLEDGMENTS
The Child's World®: Mary Berendes, Publishing Director
The Design Lab: Design and production
Red Line Editorial: Editorial direction

PHOTO CREDITS: Nancy Gill/Shutterstock Images, cover, 1, 3; Matt Kania/
Map Hero, Inc., 4, 5; Henryk Sadura/iStockphoto, 7; James Brey/iStockphoto,
9; iStockphoto, 10; Brandon Laufenberg/iStockphoto, 11; Jack Orton/AP
Images, 13; North Wind Picture Archives/Photolibrary, 15; Lawrence Sawyer/
iStockphoto, 17; AP Images, 19; Katie Derksen/AP Images, 21; One Mile Up,
22; Quarter-dollar coin image from the United States Mint, 22

LIBRARY OF CONGRESS CATALOGING-IN-PUBLICATION DATA
Saari, Holly.
 Wisconsin / by Holly Saari.
  p. cm.
 Includes bibliographical references and index.
 ISBN 978-1-60253-495-7 (library bound : alk. paper)
 1. Wisconsin—Juvenile literature. I. Title.

 F581.3.S23 2010
 977.5—dc22

                              010019916

Printed in the United States of America in Mankato, Minnesota.
July 2010
F11538

On the cover:
Wisconsin is
known for its
dairy farms.

CONTENTS

Geography

Let's explore Wisconsin! Wisconsin is in the north-central United States. This area is called the Midwest. Part of Wisconsin's northern border is Lake Superior. Wisconsin's eastern border is Lake Michigan.

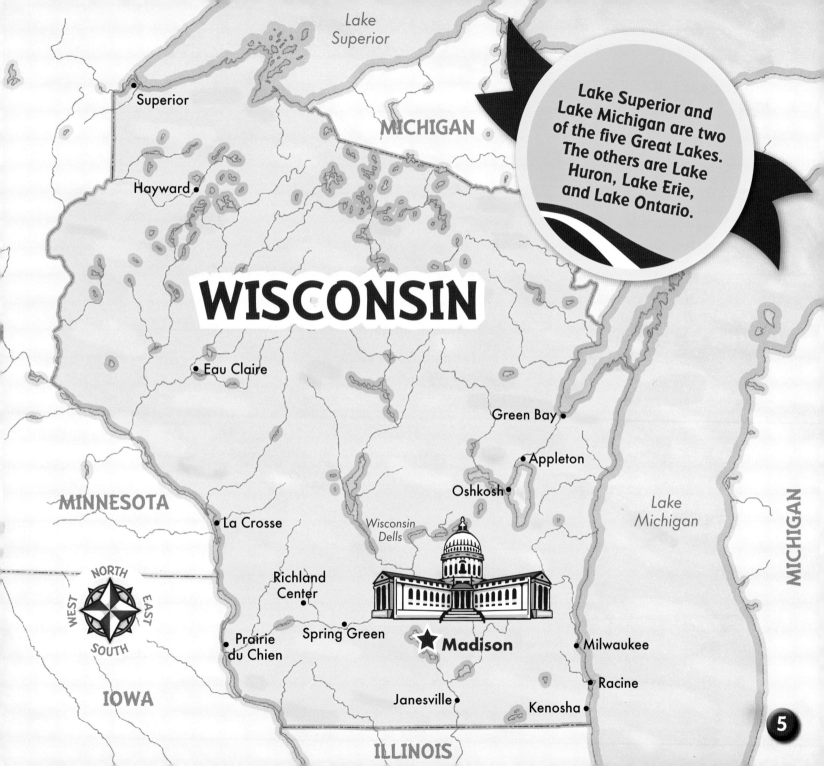

Lake
Superior

Superior

MICHIGAN

Hayward

Lake Superior and Lake Michigan are two of the five Great Lakes. The others are Lake Huron, Lake Erie, and Lake Ontario.

WISCONSIN

Eau Claire

Green Bay

Appleton

Oshkosh

MINNESOTA

La Crosse

Wisconsin
Dells

Lake
Michigan

MICHIGAN

NORTH

WEST   EAST

SOUTH

Richland
Center

Prairie
du Chien

Spring Green

★ Madison

Milwaukee

Racine

IOWA

Janesville

Kenosha

5

ILLINOIS

Cities

Madison is the capital of Wisconsin. Milwaukee is the state's largest city. Other large cities are Green Bay, Kenosha, Racine, and Appleton.

More than 570,000 people live in Milwaukee. ▶

Land

Wisconsin has many **plains**. The state also has rolling hills. Wisconsin has about 15,000 lakes. There are sandy beaches along parts of the Great Lakes.

Wisconsin's plains are good for farming. ▶

Plants and Animals

Forests cover about half of Wisconsin. The state tree is the sugar maple. The **sap** from this tree is used to make maple syrup. Animals such as deer, foxes, and badgers live in the forests. The state bird is the robin. The wood violet is the state flower.

The wood violet has purple **petals.** ▶

People and Work

More than 5.6 million people live in Wisconsin. Many people are dairy farmers. About 26 percent of the United States' cheese is made in Wisconsin. Other people make things such as paper, food products, and machines. Many people work as health-care workers or teachers. Others work in **finance** or **insurance**.

Corn, potatoes, and cranberries are important Wisconsin crops.

Wisconsin is known as "America's Dairyland." Many dairy cows are raised in the state. ▶

History

Native Americans were the first people to live in the Wisconsin area. People from Europe explored the area in the 1600s. In the 1800s, settlers began to move to the area to live. On May 29, 1848, Wisconsin became the thirtieth state.

France and England controlled the Wisconsin area before it became part of the United States.

French explorer Jean Nicolet came to the Wisconsin area in 1634. ▶

Ways of Life

Because of its many lakes, people in Wisconsin enjoy boating, fishing, and other water activities. Sports are very **popular** in the state. Many people enjoy watching college and **professional** teams. Green Bay is the smallest city in the United States to have a professional football team.

People travel to Wisconsin to take vacations and enjoy the lakes. ▶

Famous People

Artist Georgia O'Keeffe was born in Wisconsin. Laura Ingalls Wilder was born here, too. She wrote the Little House children's novels. Frank Lloyd Wright was also from Wisconsin. He **designed** buildings and houses.

Frank Lloyd Wright was born in Richland Center. He later built a famous house in Spring Green. ▶

19

Famous Places

Wisconsin Dells is a popular place to visit. This area is known for having many water parks. People also visit Wisconsin's state parks to enjoy the outdoors.

Wisconsin Dells has indoor and outdoor water parks. ▶

Visitors to Wisconsin Dells can also ride roller coasters.

State Symbols

Seal

A badger on Wisconsin's state seal stands for the state's nickname, "the Badger State." Go to **childsworld.com/links** for a link to Wisconsin's state Web site, where you can get a firsthand look at the state seal.

Flag

Wisconsin's state flag is blue with the **coat of arms** in the center. It also includes the state's name and the year Wisconsin became a state.

Quarter

Wisconsin's state quarter shows a cow, cheese, and an ear of corn. They show the importance of dairy and farm products in the state. The quarter came out in 2004.

Glossary

coat of arms (KOHT uhv ARMS): A coat of arms is a shield or other design that is a symbol for a family, state, or other group. Wisconsin's flag shows the state coat of arms.

designed (di-ZYND): If something is designed, it is carefully planned or drawn. Frank Lloyd Wright designed many houses and buildings.

finance (FYE-nanss): Finance is a group of businesses that take care of money. Some people in Wisconsin work in finance jobs.

insurance (in-SHUR-unss): Insurance is something people can buy to help them with money in case of an accident. Insurance jobs are important in Wisconsin.

petals (PET-ulz): Petals are the colorful parts of flowers. The wood violet, Wisconsin's state flower, has purple petals.

plains (PLAYNZ): Plains are areas of flat land that do not have many trees. Wisconsin has plains.

popular (POP-yuh-lur): To be popular is to be enjoyed by many people. Sports are popular in Wisconsin.

professional (pro-FESH-uh-nul): Professional means getting paid to do something that others do only for fun. Wisconsin has professional sports teams.

sap (SAP): Sap is the liquid inside a plant or tree. The sap from Wisconsin's sugar maple trees is used to make maple syrup.

seal (SEEL): A seal is a symbol a state uses for government business. Wisconsin's state seal shows a badger.

symbols (SIM-bulz): Symbols are pictures or things that stand for something else. The seal, coat of arms, and flag are Wisconsin's symbols.

Further Information

Books

Keller, Laurie. *The Scrambled States of America*. New York: Henry Holt, 2002.

Thornton, Brian. *The Everything Kids' States Book: Wind Your Way Across Our Great Nation*. Avon, MA: Adams Media, 2007.

Wargin, Kathy-jo. *B is for Badger: A Wisconsin Alphabet*. Chelsea, MI: Sleeping Bear Press, 2004.

Web Sites

Visit our Web site for links about Wisconsin: *childsworld.com/links*

Note to Parents, Teachers, and Librarians: We routinely verify our Web links to make sure they are safe and active sites. So encourage your readers to check them out!

Index